The Earth

&

The Ancestors

Ancestral Veneration Prayers

& Hoodoo Rhymes

Spiritual Black Girls

Sankofa Ancestor Shrine

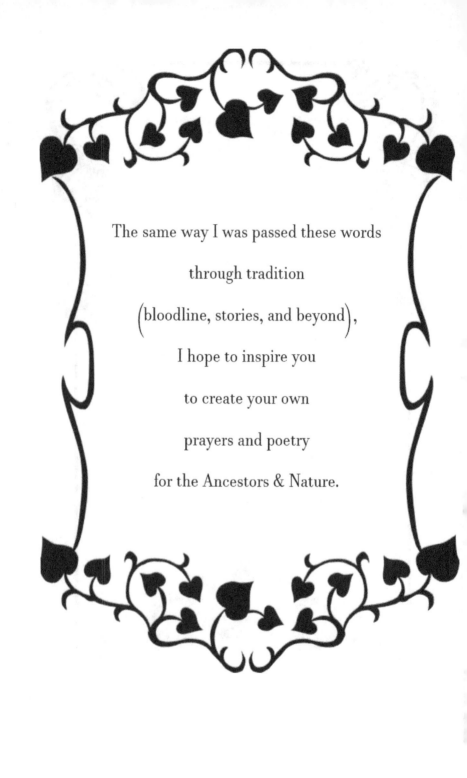

The same way I was passed these words

through tradition

(bloodline, stories, and beyond),

I hope to inspire you

to create your own

prayers and poetry

for the Ancestors & Nature.

PART ○ ONE

Prayers

Complete your prayers with *Ashe, Ayibobo, So It Is,*

So Be It, Hetepu, Amen or *Mmmm.*

Daily Prayer

May I walk this day in

Reverence.

May I walk this day in my

Center.

May I walk this day with You,

my Ancestors.

May I walk this day

Empowered by Your love.

Morning Prayer

I am thankful to the Ancestors today and

everyday.

I am excited to spread wellness this

wonderful morning.

I ask the Ancestors to assist me as I move

through each minute.

Protect me, Ancestors, and protect my

family.

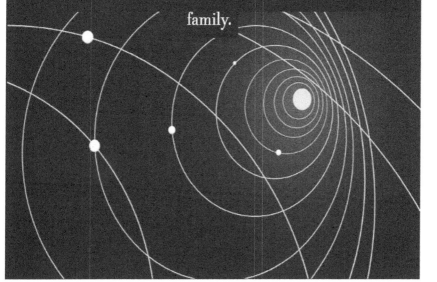

Bedtime Prayer

Now I lay myself to rest,

Pray that all the world be blessed.

As I sleep within this bed,

Ancestors, help me clear my head!

Egungun and Spirits wise;

Watch over me from deepest skies.

Mother Earth watch me until morning prayer,

Provide and keep me in your care.

Crossroads Man, protect me day and night

Bless me with courage, wisdom and insight.

And when I wake to greet the day,

Brother Sun will light the way.

Anointed By The Ancestors

My Ancestors watch over me,

They bless my every breath.

I do not worry because I know

I walk a path that's blessed.

Your Ancestors watch over you,

They bless your every breath.

Do not worry, for all of you

Walk a path that's blessed.

Prayer to A New Ancestor

You've left me for the Spirit Realm,

The cycle must go on.

And though it hurts, because I'm here

You are not really gone.

I'll see you in the flash of hope

In the brightest flower;

Your rumble will be heard in storms

That build up by the hour.

Your comfort felt as I sit

With the strength of an elder tree...

I know you have not left because

Your presence is in me.

Nature Prayer

May the Spirit of the Earth be with me.

Allow nature to remind my heart to be gentle,

my spirit be unshackled,

and my soul filled with love and kindness.

Releasing Prayer

These mountains I have carried

I was meant only to climb

Please aid me in finding vision

As I cultivate my mind.

Moon Prayer

Honor to the Moon while she is round

Luck around me be abound

Whatever I seek for shall be found

By Sea or Sky or Solid Ground.

🌙

Ancient Moon, I call you in this hour,

Fill my soul with healing power!

What I seek may it be found,

By Sea or Sky or Solid Ground!

Love and Prosperity Prayer

Spirit, help me to be a vessel for love and prosperity

coming into this world.

Your power is within me

and keeps my heart and mind centered!

Thank the Ancestors

I see what you do for me in my life;

Blessings pour over me daily nonstop.

What can I do but say thank you, Ancestors?

Please accept my thanks and gratitude,

Grant me more faith in you than ever,

That spirituality becomes central to my daily life.

Self Love

I am stars, gold and honey within this skin;

Allow me to see all the glory within.

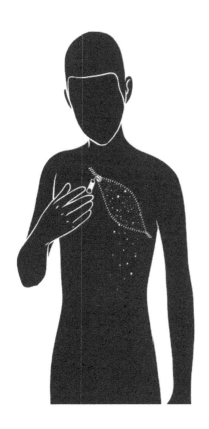

Protect My Energy Prayer

I am bright as the sun

I am high as the breeze

I breathe it all in

Cuz it's so good to me

They want to come take it

They like what they see

Don't let them get closer

Just let me be me.

Bloodline Prayer

Ancestors,

blood of my blood and bone of my bone,

my home and heart are always open to you.

I am so grateful for all that I have!

Sunrise Prayer

Reflecting at an early hour,

Inner thoughts shall give me power–

When the day comes charging through,

I will have my strength to use.

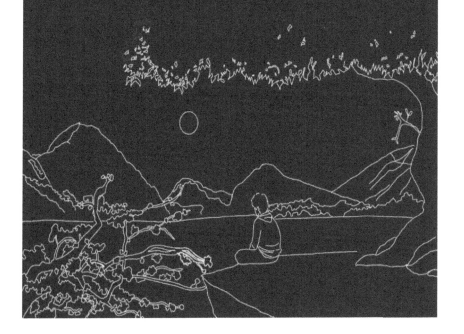

Confidence Prayer

The Sacred Eye,

Spiritual might,

May I always know

What comes in Sight.

Something enters–

I will see,

And then react

Accordingly.

When wisdom and

knowledge

Reveal their face,

I know I can

Adapt with grace.

Others falter,

Perhaps confused,

I will always

Discern the cues.

I do not hold

An ounce of fear

To use my strength

Or shed a tear.

For whatever future

Comes my way

My Ancestors stand

With me always.

Perseverance

There's a fire within me

That I must let burn,

Please give me the strength

To overcome my concerns.

Protection Prayer

Ancestor's of my

Bloodline——

Wild, strong and free!

Protect me, my home,

and those I love

For all eternity!

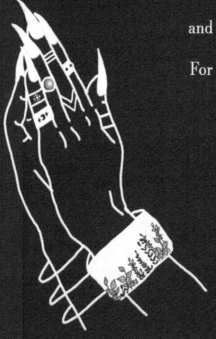

Self Protection Prayer

I call on my Ancestors

both known and unknown!

Bless those who bless me,

curse those who curse me,

and may love and prosperity

be brought to my home!

Family Protection Prayer

May my family tree be healed/protected

from what troubles us

as I focus with intention on our love and the

connection we share.

I have faith in knowing the Ancestors will

heal us, sending this energy back to us in

return!

Crossroads

Ancestors! May your guidance and wisdom
continue to be a path opener for me and mine and
remain with me at every crossroads.

Land Blessing

Honor to the sacred energy of the Land!

Honor to the flora, fauna, waters, and skies!

Honor to Muva Earth!

Honor the Ancestors

Ancestors,

I fear nothing with you at my side.

I honor you in my home & heart

and from the roots deep in the soil

to the skies high above!

Food Offering

Ancestors, We give invite all the spirits of our tribe to partake! Here is our food, made by our hands with our ingredients... Receive it and look after your family.

Defend your children against danger! Let what is bad go with the setting sun and give us health and wealth.

Tree Prayer

Sacred Gateway on Mama Earth——

Protectors and Providers, I call on your power!

Help me to grow to towering heights, and sink my roots

deep wherever I stand.

You who builds homes, creates fire, and spreads

knowledge

Protect me through all the storms of life!

Empower me with the miraculous power of the seed,

The creative reach and growth of the leaves and branches,

And the nourishment and sturdiness of the trunk.

Grant me longevity, wellness and strength, Soul Protector

I call on your power!

New Home Blessing

Here we stand and bless the threshold,

Stepping into the new with a faith that's bold.

Ancestors, support us for every tomorrow,

Give us much joy and comfort us in our sorrows.

Cleanse this space, remove the past.

We've found our happy home at last.

Clear anything destructive that's been here

Let all but goodness disappear!

Heal the energy within this place;

Bring us love, protection and grace.

Fill this home with joy and love;

And send us blessings from above.

House Blessing

Ancestors, bless this home!

May only good fortune and safe journeys bless friends

who walk through this door.

Thank you for this stable place to stand, for these four

walls which house our love and laughter!

May the roof hold strong and these roots reach deep,

And may we be comforted and protected when we go to

sleep.

I banish all evil and negativity from this home. Only

good shall prosper here!

May this home be blessed.

Leaving Home Prayer

Thank you for protecting me for all this time.

In this home let love abide

And bless those who soon will live inside.

Please accept this small offering as a token of my gratitude.

(flowers, coins, art etc.)

Mama Earth Reconnection Prayer

Mama! Earth! My helper, healer, and most powerful
teacher.

I put my feet into your soil and take these moments to
remember all the ways we interact every day that I may
forget or look over in my haste.

I remember in gratitude you, my Great Mother, who

sustains me and all of us on the planet.

I remember in gratitude the Sun high above, which gives

us daylight and helps the plants grow.

I also give thanks to the Moon and Stars, which shine so

bright when the Sun is gone, the Moon moving the tides

and seas below.

I remember with gratitude the Winds and Sky which bring

new seeds and change.

I am thankful for the Clouds, the Rains, the Rivers, Streams

and Oceans, the natural cycle which gives us water.

Returned thanks to the plants which heal us and sustain us,

house us and teach us

And I return thanks to you, Mama Earth! I renew my

promise to protect you and continue to be a student who

learns of your ways as I continue my life's journey.

Mother Earth

I pray to you, Mother Earth, to show   our appreciation!

I am grateful for all that you provide for sustenance and

creation!

I pray to you, Mother Earth, to remind myself to be

humble...

Help me to remember I am a small part of a larger

picture, and how my actions impact the world beyond my

own life.

I ask you to continue to teach us, sustain us, and allow us to take our place rightfully as caretakers of your bounty.

Help me to understand my place and to remain inspired to continue to do my part!

I pray to you, Mother Earth, to help me remember to be a voice.

Make me a voice for those who cannot speak! Help me to be a voice for what I know is right. Help me to not be silent in moments that require me to speak, and to not agree in moments where I am pressured against my morals and better judgement.

I pray also, Mother Earth, asking for forgiveness.

Through both ignorance and deliberate choices, I have harmed you, been wasteful of resources, and taken for granted what you provide (harming not only myself, but others, including my own descendents).

Give me the strength and fortitude to help care for and save the planet!

☾

Mother Earth, please continue to hold and sustain us!

Make me a guardian of your waters and mountains and air!

Help me understand the importance of each of your parts-- no matter how large or small!

Mother Earth, please continue to hold and sustain us!

Make me a guardian of your waters and mountains and air!

Help me understand the importance of each of your parts-- no matter how large or small!

Make me Nature's advocate, teach me of your stillness and help me root out suffering to replace with security.

Prayer for a Child

Ancestors, bless this child,

Bless their breath

Bless their spirit

Heart of my heart,

Your wildest dreams,

Bless the continuation of our bloodline!

Baby Blessings

◎ Ancestors, give constant protection and grant a

healthy birth.

◎ Let the Ancestors be with you and give you peace.

◎ Ancestors, guard and protect them.

◎ Bless this child's room and keep them in your sight.

◎ May the Ancestors keep you safe.

◎ May you have a long and healthy life.

◎ I speak Ancestral blessings over you,

◎ May your eyes look ahead towards the future.

◎ May you always prosper and be in good health.

Insomniac's Prayer

I pray the Ancestors take my face

Wrap my body pure with lace

Make me libations poured in vase

To consecrate and bless this place.

I pray to you within the night

Let my manifestations take true flight.

Am I wrong or am I right?

My bloodline gives me true insight.

Take my words and make them right.

Let my intentions

have inner Sight——

What inspiring thoughts happen be

Let them be created instantaneously.

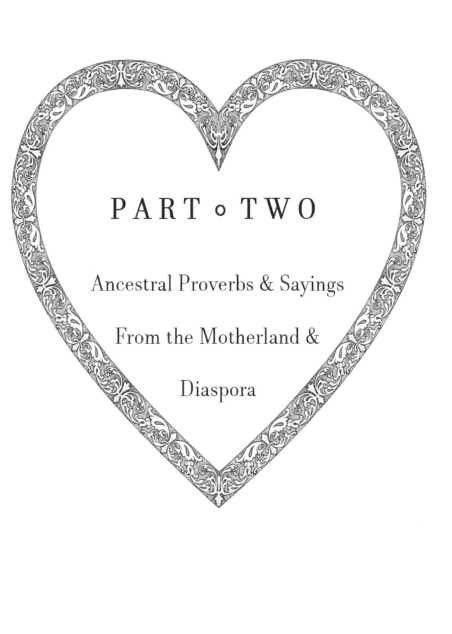

PART ○ TWO

Ancestral Proverbs & Sayings

From the Motherland &

Diaspora

A proverb is the horse that can carry one swiftly to the

discovery of ideas.

Yoruba Proverb

"I am not African because I was born in Africa but

because Africa was born in me."

Kwame Nkrumah

Always being in a hurry does not prevent death, neither

does going slowly prevent living.

Igbo Proverb

"You are either alive and proud or you are dead, and

when you are dead, you can't care anyway."

Steve Biko

Silent river run deep.

Jamaican Proverb

Knowledge is not the main thing, but deeds.

Sierra Leonean Proverb

If given stew, add water; you must be wiser than the

cook.

Yoruba Proverb

One does not enter into the water and then run from

the cold.

Yoruba Proverb

Knowledge is like a garden: if it is not cultivated, it

cannot be harvested.

Unknown

Perform good deeds; you will not regret them.

Moroccan Proverb

If the owner of a calabash calls it a worthless calabash,

others will join him to use it to pack rubbish.

Nigerian Proverb

One does not engage in a dyeing trade in Isokun; people

there wear only white.

Yoruba Proverb

"Proverbs are the palm oil with which words are eaten."

Chinua Achebe

Even the mightiest eagle comes down to the treetops to

rest.

Ugandan Proverb

Riches are found in cultivating together.

Bajan Proverb

One does not fight to save another person's head only to

have one's own carried away.

Yoruba Proverb

Every mickle mek a muckle.

Jamaican Proverb

One does not compete with another for a chieftaincy title

and also show your competitor the way to the king's house.

Yoruba Proverb

A bag that says it will not take more, and a traditional

doctor who says they will not leave anything behind are

both sure to suffer.

Nigerian Proverb

One does not leave one elder sitting to walk another elder

part of his way.

Yoruba Proverb

When a head is too big it cannot avoid punches.

Zambian Proverb

Nobody can see his own goodness: it can be seen only by

others.

Bajan Proverb

"For Africa to me... is more than a glamorous fact. It is a

historical truth. No man can know where he is going unless

he knows exactly where he has been and exactly how he

arrived at his present place."

Maya Angelou

Tomorrow is pregnant and no-one knows what she will give birth to.

Eritrean Proverb

One does not dive underwater without knowing how to swim.

Yoruba Proverb

Trouble nuh set like rain.

Jamaican Proverb

One does not use oneself as an ingredient in a medicine requiring that the ingredients be pulverized.

Yoruba Proverb

It is not only the fox, even the snail arrives at its

destination.

Nigerian Proverb

One does not leave cloth in a bundle while bargaining

over it.

Yoruba Proverb

"While revolutionaries as individuals can be murdered,

you cannot kill ideas."

Thomas Sankara

One does not ignore leprosy to treat a rash.

Yoruba Proverb

Remember that it is the same moon that wanes today that

will be full tomorrow.

Nigerian Proverb

"Service to others is the rent you pay for your room here

on earth."

Muhammad Ali

One does not use a sword to kill a snail.

Yoruba Proverb

The siever never sifts flour by itself.

Yoruba Proverb

One does not as a joke say one's mother has collapsed.

Yoruba Proverb

A farmer who would not work inside the rain and would

not work under the sun will have nothing to harvest at the

end of the farming year.

Nigerian Proverb

One does not hide something in one's hand and yet swear

that one knows nothing about it.

Yoruba Proverb

"One of the truest tests of integrity is its blunt refusal

to be compromised."

Chinua Achebe

"If you are neutral in situations of injustice, you have chosen the side of the oppressor. If an elephant has its foot on the tail of a mouse and you say that you are neutral, the mouse will not appreciate your neutrality."

Desmond Tutu

One does not make a gift of someone else's property.

Yoruba Proverb

If the rhythm of the drum beat changes, the dance step must adapt.

Kenyan Proverb

One does not consume salt according to one's greatness.

Yoruba Proverb

The wisdom of the elderly is like the sun, it illuminates

the whole village.

Ugandan Proverb

Evil counsel is the root of misfortune.

Hausa Proverb

One does not show the throat the way to the stomach.

Yoruba Proverb

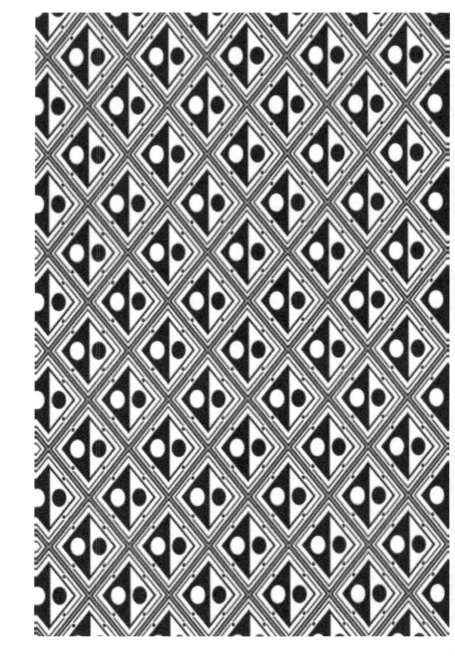

If familiarity were always useful, water wouldn't
cook fish.

Cameroonian Proverb

Do not abuse midwives while there is a delivery

Swahili Proverb

It is not right for a race horse to despise the pace

of a pony.

Hausa Proverb

One does not grab hold of a person who has

pulled a knife.

Yoruba Proverb

Education is life, not books.

Swahili Proverb

A lie can annihilate a thousand truths.

Ashanti Proverb

Where hands are needed, words and letters are useless.

Nigerian Proverb

One does not throw a toad away, then inquire

after its young.

Yoruba Proverb

What is hanging high up, cannot be reached while sitting

down.

Cameroonian Proverb

A youth that does not cultivate friendship with the elderly

is like a tree without roots.

Ugandan Proverb

"[Fight] so that future generations will have the resources

and assets they need to survive on a planet that's being

destroyed every day."

Miriam Miranda

It is not worth talking about a slip of the foot as if it were

a fall.

Efik Proverb

One does not carve a tall statue without resting its hand

on something.

Yoruba Proverb

If you have a lot, give some of your possessions; if you

have little give some of your heart.

Ugandan Proverb

In every head is some wisdom.

Egyptian Proverb

One does not collect water from a spring to dump

in the deep.

Yoruba Proverb

If you destroy a bridge, be sure you can swim.

Swahili Proverb

One should not expect flight from the flightless chicken;

one should not expect striding from a chameleon.

Yoruba Proverb

Even today, the remedy for dirt is water.

Hausa Proverb

To go where there is no road is better than to remain

without doing anything.

Wolof Proverb

It takes a lot of work; it's not a sprint. But it's achievable

if we view it as important.

Robert Bullard, European American Environmentalist

Who walks in the mud, at some point must

clean their feet.

Kenyan Proverb

One does not deliver a verdict after hearing only one side.

Yoruba Proverb

"Believe in the power of building communities to stop the problems we face."

Kibiriti Majuto, Activist

If you collect peppers one by one, the plant grows well; but if you break the stem, it dies.

Akan Proverb

The stick in the hand is the one that kills the snake

Swahili Proverb

One does not eat I almost in a stew.

Yoruba Proverb

A wealthy person is a selfish person.

Ovambo Proverb

"[Have] the life of a man who knows that the world is

not given by his fathers, but borrowed from his children;

who has undertaken to cherish it and do it no damage,

not because he is duty-bound, but because he loves the

world and loves his children

Wendell Berry, American Environmentalist

Those who farm little, harvest less.

Akan Proverb

When a fly does not get up off a dead body, he is buried

with it.

Ashanti Proverb

A person who is not disciplined cannot be cautioned

Swahilian Proverb

One does not count a god's grove as part of the town.

Yoruba Proverb

Where there is no shame, there is no honor.

Cameroonian Proverb

"Education, if it means anything, should not take people away from the land, but instill in them even more respect for it, because educated people are in a position to understand what is being lost. The future of the planet concerns all of us, and all of us should do what we can to protect it. As I told the foresters, and the women, you don't need a diploma to plant a tree."

Wangari Maathai, Environmentalist

One does not count a fetus among living children.

Yoruba Proverb

A masquerade is not a spirit only because of its mask.

Nigerian Proverb

One does not have children at one's rear

and yet refuse food.

Yoruba Proverb

"History is your future."

Beyonce

"Our existing on this planet is everything. There's nothing

more important. That's why I fight."

Antonique Smith, Artivist

One does not devote oneself to the home and devote oneself

to the farm and not wind up neglecting one of them.

Yoruba Proverb

"Police violence is an aspect of a broader pattern of structural violence, which the climate crisis is a manifestation of. Healing structural violence is actually in the best interest of all human beings."

Sam Grant, Environmentalist

One does not have a thousand cowries at home and go chasing abroad for a thousand cowries.

Yoruba Proverb

One does not kill the vulture; one does not eat the vulture; one does not offer the vulture as a sacrifice to one's head.

Yoruba Proverb

"I watch the blue jays, 50 or more, that come down each day swooping easily from limb to limb with raucous laughter, feet curled under. And in the quiet I hear the voice of the river passing among the rocks and over stones, everywhere at once, making its way through steep green canyons to the sea. I try to catch the words mingling with the shushing of the trees. Perhaps this is where our speech began. Maybe long ago before there were words, there was only the river and the people listened to the water...and the quiet whispering."

John Francis, Planetwalker

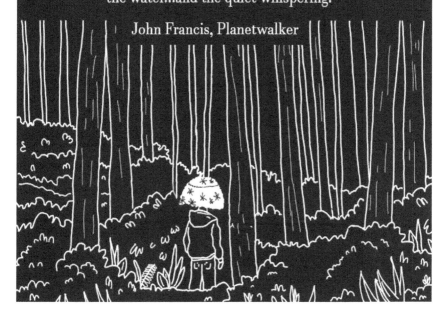

One does not dare a wicked person to do their worst.

Yoruba Proverb

The cobra that blocks the path is going his own way, yet

people run away when they see him.

Akan Proverb

One does not send a shirker to go see what the morning

looks like outside.

Yoruba Proverb

It is ineptitude in setting it down that makes the wine for

the egun spill.

Yoruba Proverb

"That ability to see what is unseen and to hope, and to really feel what it's like to be in the wishful future is I think a superpower that everybody has. And I think we all do better and do more, and do it with more joy when we're living in the future that we want."

Heather McGhee, Political Commentator

One does not see chickens about and throw one's corn to the dog.

Yoruba Proverb

He who refuses to obey cannot command.

Kenyan Proverb

Everyone deserves to eat safe food, drink safe water, have

their kids play outside safely."

Robert Bullard

If your mouth turns into a knife, it will cut off your lips.

Zimbabwean Proverb

One does not see a bata drum on the ground and use one's

mouth to mimic its sound.

Yoruba Proverb

Wisdom is like fire. People take it from others.

Hema Proverb

Tortoise says there is nothing quite like

what one knows how to do;

it says when it walks through a peanut farm,

peanuts keep popping one by one into its mouth.

Yoruba Proverb

The monkey does not see his own hind parts;

he sees his neighbor's.

Zimbabwean Proverb

One does not find helpers willing to help with one's load

and yet sprout a hump on one's back "from carrying too

heavy a load".

Yoruba Proverb

He who learns, teaches.

Ethiopian Proverb

One does not wallow in poverty and yet kill an elephant

public distribution.

Yoruba Proverb

Unfinished abandoned wall: unable to master it, one

befriends it.

Yoruba Proverb

A needle cannot be used to make pounded yams.

Yoruba Proverb

He who disappoints teaches one to be more resourceful.

Yoruba Proverb

The parasite is destroying itself, but it thinks it is

destroying its host.

Yoruba Proverb

Wisdom is not like money to be tied up and hidden.

Akan proverb

It is wicked when an elder sows suffering for their

children.

Yoruba Proverb

It is completely and securely that a mother supports the

child with a strip of cloth on her back.

Yoruba Proverb

A person who knows how to wash his hands

will eat with elders.

Yoruba Proverb

And the wind said, "May you be as strong as the oak, yet flexible as the birch, may you stand as tall as the redwood, live gracefully as the willow and may you always bear fruit all your days on this earth."

Unknown

Neglect to say, "Here is your's" is what incites the earth's

anger.

Yoruba Proverb

The person who eats large helpings does not care that

there is a famine.

Yoruba Proverb

When rain beats on a leopard it wets him, but it does not

wash out his spots.

Ashanti Proverb

It is the leavings from his table that the farmer sells.

Yoruba Proverb

A stranger has eyes, but they do not see.

Yoruba Proverb

One twig will not sweep.

Hausa Proverb

The journey is never so pleasant that the parrot does not

return to Iwo.

Yoruba Proverb

The wielder of the incantation rattle lifts it, and you

respond, "May it be so!";

do you know if he has invoked good or evil?

Yoruba Proverb

A person who rises in the morning without washing his

face, one who sees things with yesterday's eyes.

Yoruba Proverb

The elephant is impossible to carry.

Yoruba Proverb

When it rains, the roof always drips the same way

Jabo Proverb

The person who beats the drum must also know the

song.

Bemba Proverb

"As you walk look around, assess where you are,

reflect on where you have been, and dream of

where you are going. Every moment of the

present contains the seeds of opportunity for

change. Your life is an adventure. Live it fully."

John Francis, Planetwalker

When the spider wants to engage an enemy, it spins its web around it.

Yoruba Proverb

The person with the crossbow thinks that the monkey is not clever; the monkey is clever, but it is following its own strategy.

Yoruba Proverb

The new moon cannot come until the other has gone.

Ugandan Proverb

A stranger who asks the way will not get lost.

Yoruba Proverb

One does not become a master diviner in a day. A forest is not made in a season. The swoop of an eagle has seen many seasons and floods.

Nigerian Proverb

"Many of us forget that this work is long term. It isn't an overnight fix, and we have to prepare the next line of fighters for the work. I had to become my own advocate...Once I created what I needed, I reached back to help others like me. In that reach back, I realized that I had to move out of the way."

Quentin Bell, Activist

The person who knew the way last year does not

necessarily know the way this year.

Yoruba Proverb

Always taking out without giving back, even the

mountains will be broken down.

Libyan Proverb

By the time the fool has learned the game, the players

have dispersed.

Ashanti Proverb

The old person who incurs debt, he says how much of it

will he be around to pay?

Yoruba Proverb

You are not born a leader, you become one.

Cameroonian Proverb

The world goes forth, and we follow.

Yoruba Proverb

The seed that is sown is the one that sprouts.

Hausa Proverb

"A lot of times we find ourselves in this wonderful place where we've gotten to, but there is another place for us to go & we kind of have to leave behind the security of who we've become and go to the place who we are becoming."

John Francis, Planetwalker

To love the king is not bad, but a king who loves you is better.

Wolof Proverb

He who spies on others from behind their walls upsets himself.

Yoruba Proverb

What you help a child to love can be more important than what you help him to learn.

Unknown

If one's head was a pot and one gave it to an enemy to inspect, he would say it was irretrievably broken.

Yoruba Proverb

Indecision is like the stepchild: if he doesn't wash his hands, he is called dirty; if he does, he is wasting the water.

Malagasy Proverb

A child does not naturally understand codes.

Yoruba Proverb

The world is not a thing to
exchange threats with; it can
inflict disaster on one.

Yoruba Proverb

The world does not deserve to be trusted; if you have a
store of wisdom, keep it in you.

Yoruba Proverb

One who applies proverbs gets what they want.

Shona Proverb

PART ○ THREE

Stars & Rush & Melanin:

Hoodoo Rhymes

Advice

Smoke the room to start the day, all your troubles

melt away

Allow the flora grow with care, and this abundance

will be shared

Your curls adorn with softest touch, and they shall

grow ever much.

Use your crystals every night, allow your dreams to

take true flight.

Feel comfort in your melanin; your Ancestors will

help you win.

Sacred

Spirit shows us what is Sacred——

Intuition helps us know the way.

We lose our power when we give the Sacred

To just any curious face.

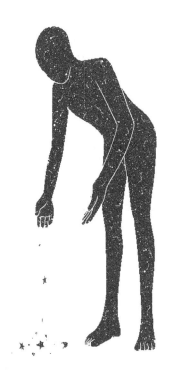

When people ask to

understand

The things we keep away

I let them know this

knowledge is

For my bloodline only.

Blessed

My life has exactly the

Flavor I crave–

I will not change a thing

Till I'm locked in my grave.

Growth

We may grow strong as oak,

Or as soft as the fern,

But in the end growth is a lesson

That all of us learn.

Imposter Syndrome

I try so hard to find my peace,

But the other side is just in reach.

Its nastiness holds a comfort grip...

I keep my vigilance, lest I slip.

I do not know which side will win–

Both people fit within my skin.

Faith

I don't try to break it down–

Rootwork isn't quite that way;

I just let it wrap around me

And believe the words I pray.

Us

You have that certain kind of magic——

It rumbles deep within your core,

That insists upon my essence,

And forces me to crave you more.

Relationship

You humble yourself for me,

And I'm grateful that you do.

I know that very few receive

This same treatment from you.

When I return the favor,

It continues on what we've built...

Our bond is warm, yet intricate

Just like a home- made quilt.

Strength & Weakness

I cannot help

But take a peek

Into the mirror

Before I sleep.

My resolve is strong

But my past is weak.

I tie my hair

And start to speak.

My prayer exits,

Calm and meek:

Please give me strength

To take that leap.

Keep Going

All receive hurts and journeys and dreams,

And have things turn out

Not as they first seemed.

We each are presented with

An uncertain path,

To always walk forward

And learn from our past.

Lay Hands

Rub hands together,

Create the heat

Build the energy

Where palms meet

The energy I transfer

Comes through me each day.

I make changes around me

With the words that I say.

Divine

A mania blesses the core–

A willingness to thrill;

The feminine//masculine within me

Threatens to overspill.

Hands droop lazy

To loyalty's abyss...

Infinity of possibility

Is what gives me bliss.

Discipline

I allow the thoughts to slip

through my mind

While automatic

proceedings dictate this

grind. If I am to live the life

that I deserve,I must be

wary of the choices I serve.

African Traditional Religion

Power churns beneath our skin

Stars and rush and melanin

Tradition's distinctly African

Pushing forward just to win

It's not accidental our ways are their sins

And religions condemned as the devil within,

But it's our duty not to abandon those who have

been——

To pour libations with water, whisky and gin

And keep alive Ancient knowledge that dwells

therein.

Self Reflection

I try to speak before I break

I always dream before I wake

I mold this mind, I move, I make

I consider before each step I take.

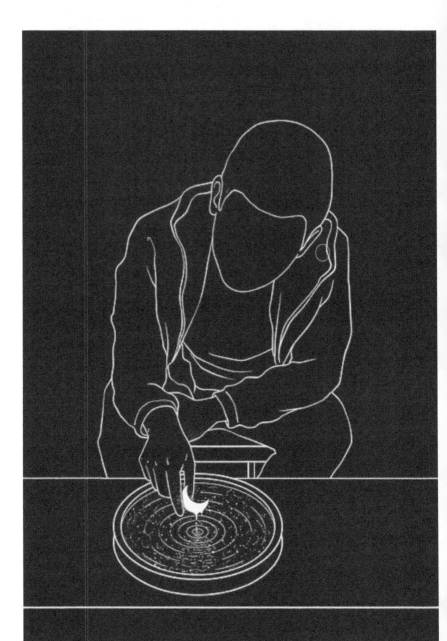

Garden

Place it in a shallow pit.

Smooth the good Earth over it.

And when the rains come tumbling down

Bless the soil, deep and brown.

From the rising to the setting sun

When the air from the four winds has begun

May the plants rise strong, may my knowledge grow

May Mama Earth bless this place and all I sow.

RitualReady.com

Youtube & Patreon:

Sankofa Ancestor Shrine

Made in the USA
Las Vegas, NV
15 March 2024

87239433R00079